From Darkness to Light
A Journey Through Depression

Compiled by Sam Choo

First Published 2023 by Hope Publishing

ISBN No. 978-981-18-7831-2

Contact Email: sam@hopepublishing.sg

Contents

Introduction 4

My Shadow Friend (by Why Keen) 6

I Drown No More but Soar Higher and Higher (by Olukemi Awodokun) 15

Journey of Learning about Depression (by Jimmy Tan San Tek) 19

A Journey Into Health & Happiness (by Jessica See) 24

My Story of Depression (by Tamikio Dooley) 34

Embracing the Sunlight Within (by Faranaz Mahmood Khan) 38

Highly Functional Depression (by Lee Li Li) 44

The Cries Within (by Hadi Al Maatiin) 58

The Optimistic Surface (by Anna Ng) 66

Rising from the Shadows (by Carollyne Tong) 77

Overcoming Depression after Losing my Dad (by Hisham Ahmad) 87

Work in Progress (by Fazal Ahamed) 91

From Darkness I Saw Light (by Rajalakshmi Jeyabalan) ... 98

You are GOOD enough! (by Allie Ng) 105

This Palette of Madness (by Janice Sheilah) 115

Introduction

"From darkness to light: A journey through depression" is a book that tells the personal stories of people who have experienced depression, and how they have triumphed over it. The book shares their struggles, but also highlights their resilience in overcoming their challenges. It offers hope and inspiration to others who may be going through similar experiences. This book is for anyone who wants to learn more about depression and how to cope with it.

We share these stories not just as a testimony of personal triumph, but as an encouragement to others who may find themselves in similar situations. Remember, you are not alone, and there is always hope.

If you are struggling, I urge you to:

Seek support from friends, family, or professionals. Don't be afraid to open up and share your feelings and challenges.

Stay connected with your faith and maintain your spiritual practices, such as prayer and meditation.

Focus on your passions and interests, and explore new opportunities for personal and professional growth.

Surround yourself with positive influences and eliminate negativity from your life.

Remember that setbacks are temporary, and with determination and perseverance, you can overcome them and soar higher.

Together, we can create a world where everyone is supported, understood, and empowered to reach their full potential, regardless of their circumstances. Let us continue to uplift one another, celebrate our successes, and work towards a more inclusive and compassionate society.

Stay strong, have faith, and never give up. Your best days are ahead, and you are destined to soar higher and higher.

My Shadow Friend

By Why Keen

I want to share something that I recently discovered about myself and my struggles for the past few years. I am quite sure I have depression. It is not exactly a secret; I share this openly with close friends and family. Sharing helps with management, but what was important for me was inward observation and mindful practice in my daily life.

I've always believed that there's a counterbalance to everything we think and do; every yin (negative) has a yang (positive). This belief was super helpful in my discovery of the concept of a "Shadow Friend."

I realised that my depression was not just about the outward symptoms but also a hidden dark self within me that I had unknowingly created over the years. This dark self was the opposite of the persona I presented to the world and was kept secret, hidden in the shadows.

It was only through observation and reflection on my thoughts and behaviors that I noticed this "Shadow Friend" and the destructive impact of this hidden dark self on my mental well-being. It was like a parallel version of me, but one that I had ignored for so long.

Every one of us has a "Shadow Friend"; try to observe this. This friend lies behind our thoughts, our judgment on the world, and will remain hidden unless we know he/she is there.

Let's try an example of a strong, independent CEO of an MNC, Ms. Indie. Ms. Indie is a powerhouse at her workplace and a perfect mother. She takes pride in being independent and self-sufficient. Whenever she has self-doubts, she tells herself, "Come on, you've got this. You are strong!" Each time she tells herself this, her mirrored self, the little girl in her who feels anxious and helpless, gets suppressed. Let's call this girl Anxiety.

When all is well and good, Anxiety is hidden from the world, but what happens in a crisis?

In a crisis, Ms. Indie's mirrored self, Anxiety, the little girl who feels anxious and helpless, may come out in full force. The usual coping mechanisms and self-assurances that Ms. Indie relies on may not be as effective in the face of a crisis. The pressure and challenges of the situation may trigger the underlying insecurities and fears of Anxiety.

Because Ms. Indie has not acknowledged nor addressed the needs of her mirrored self, she may not be able to handle a crisis. When Anxiety comes out in full force, she can only despair. She can feel like there is nothing left to do, and that's when depression sets in.

Ms. Indie probably didn't even know there was a "Shadow Friend" growing inside her. Anxiety had been demanding attention and care, and ignoring her needs may exacerbate the crisis and hinder Ms. Indie's ability to cope.

So how do we manage this "Shadow Friend"? I managed to find an answer for myself. I would share it here, hoping that it provides some understanding for your own journey.

Step 1 - Mindfulness
I need to start by saying that it took quite a long time for me to practice mindfulness and become comfortable with sitting with my emotions. This journey took years, but it started there.

It is quite impossible to share the entire practice of mindfulness in a few short paragraphs, so I won't. But I would share one of the concepts I learnt, which was the illusion of self.

We were all brought up to believe that we are one person, with the same beliefs, the same character, one consistent being, but is that necessarily true? Dig a little deeper, and you will notice that this may not be true. How many times have we scolded ourselves? Retroactively saying, "Why was I so stupid to do that?" after making a decision we regret or said something to others like "I couldn't control myself."

In observing my thoughts and emotions, especially when I am in a bad state, I found that I may not be the same person. So the practice of mindfulness helped me with observing that my representation of self is truly just an illusion.

Step 2 - Observation
The second thing I had to do was notice my friend. I also call him my roommate because he is always there in the same room that is my mind with me. Picture sharing a room with a sibling. This visualization helped me greatly.

I would start to notice when I began feeling a familiar emotion due to some triggers. It could be anger, it could be sadness. I learned to recognize these feelings as a sign that my "Shadow Friend" needed something.

Step 3 - Compassion
The third step was just to sit with my friend. That was it. No judgment, no scolding like the example I

gave above, just being with him. It meant accepting anything that was already done, as done. It meant allowing any feelings to come, to come.

This is a powerful thing that we can do for our friends who might need us for emotional support too, and I mean, real, physical friends this time! Part of my entire healing process was when friends were able to do this for me. One of my best friends called me after I posted something I was going through on Facebook, and he was concerned for me. He didn't offer solutions, he didn't tell me I should stop thinking too much, he just asked if he could buy me a meal and hang out. When we did hang out, he was just there, as a friend, as I was processing my emotions.

So for my "Shadow Friend", I did just that. Sit, and be a friend. In time, he began to reveal who he was.

Practically, what this meant was me noticing that I couldn't function very well in certain situations anymore, stepping away for a while, and doing something that I liked in a space I felt comfortable and safe in. It meant telling my wife and family what I was going through at the moment, and asking for that space.

It meant realizing that my "Shadow Friend" needed something, and knowing with experience not to ignore it or risk aggravating the problem. If I were to power through and ignore the pain, I could, and I did do that for years. It is like when you are having a high fever and diarrhea and still needing to cover a wedding as their videographer! It is possible, but it just means you are causing damage that takes a bit longer to recover from each time.

So picture me, usually health-conscious, and usually thrifty with my own needs, splurging money on exquisite ice cream and sitting in front of the TV watching a comedy.

Step 4 - Understanding
Everything up to this point was just establishing a trusting, loving relationship with my mirrored self. Step 4 was then slowly understanding him.

I gave an example of an independent Ms. Indie, proud of her strength as a superwoman coming to realize her "Shadow Self" was Anxiety, a little girl who was really anxious all the time. Her confident exterior had a mirrored anxiousness that is equal in strength residing in her "Shadow Self."

In my own version, it was not easy figuring out what my own "Shadow Self" wanted. You see, the problem is that this part of ourselves is usually the opposite of an attribute we are proud of and forms our identity, or the illusion of one.

What our "Shadow Self" wants is usually very shameful, and something we ignore or suppress in ourselves. It might even be something we hate about ourselves. If you noticed, I am still hesitant to share my own "Shadow Self" now, because I am honestly still too embarrassed to reveal this. It's like I have a racist uncle in the family I would not tell other people about.

However, I remember the moment I understood my roommate. I had a very profound feeling of joy. It explained so many things. Why do I get triggered by this? Why did I feel so happy when that happened? It was like I found an instruction manual to my brain.

Step 5 - Yang to the Yin

Step 5 was the beginning of healing. Now that I understood my roommate, I created an equally powerful yang to his yin. I provided unconditional love and acknowledgement to his existence. I did not reject him or scold him for being a certain way, because remember, the more we push something away, the harder it comes back?

It meant looking at my shame and saying, "It's ok. I love you all the same."

For Ms. Indie (see how I keep using an example, instead of my own?), it meant feeling anxious before a meeting with the board of directors and acknowledging that feeling. It meant telling Anxiety, "I see your fear, it is normal to feel this way, but we will get through this." It meant knowing when to take a break when overwhelmed with too many decisions in her day, acknowledging that she is only human.

It doesn't diminish her confidence in any way if her counter acknowledgment of her anxiety is equally strong, instead, a balance of sorts is found.

Conclusion

So that was what I went through. Healing began only when I started acknowledging and addressing the hidden dark self with self-awareness and self-compassion. It wasn't easy, but it was a crucial step towards improving my mental health.

I want to encourage anyone who's struggling with depression or any other mental health challenge to dig deeper and uncover if there's a mirrored self within you. It is not about blaming ourselves, but rather about understanding and managing the hidden dark self with kindness and care.

Remember, sharing with friends and family was a major part of the process too. We can feel lonely while still acknowledging that we are not alone in this journey, and there is hope for healing and growth.

Let's strive towards a more balanced and authentic version of ourselves.

About Why Keen

Why Keen is a seasoned professional in advertising and a skilled storyteller. As CEO and Creative Director of a successful social media platform, he brought unique stories to life. Through his blog and art, Why Keen continues to captivate readers with his enigmatic aura and unique perspective. https://www.whykeen.com

I Drown No More but Soar Higher and Higher

By Olukemi Awodokun

Some time ago, I was jobless, lonely, and hopeless. I was very depressed and lost hope in everything, not just because of my situation at the time but also because of people's attitudes towards me. Mind you, I was already a university graduate at the time.

Days when there would be no food to eat.

Days when I would wake up in the morning with no one to talk to and no other choice but to stay indoors from dawn to dusk.

Days when I just wondered if I was good enough to be anyone's friend.

Days when I tried to do some business to make ends meet, but nothing seemed to align or add up.

Days when I felt guilty for not being the best that I

should be, but I tried – the results just weren't forthcoming...

In our society, people tend to knock down those who are already down. This is when some insensitive individuals deem it appropriate to make snide comments under the guise of 'care'. "Why do you have to waste money buying sewing machines? You should have gone back to school to study Nursing instead of 'wasting' your money on sewing machines!" – this is just one of many comments I received! A terrible experience!

I was in that situation for more than two years! But one thing kept me going – the assurance that God had not forgotten me. I am a Christian, I had served God with my life and my all, so I knew 'God WILL NOT forsake me now that I need Him'.

God spoke to me regularly, and no matter what, I never stopped praying and believing. God didn't allow my situation to overwhelm me. The constant reminder that God was with me and He loved me served as my motivation in the face of depression. That is how I was able to rise above the thoughts that nearly pulled me down.

Another thing I consciously did was to speak up. I spoke to an older friend. Thankfully, she listened and provided great help. I didn't keep it all to myself.

We were able to trace the events that led to my sad situation; from bad business strategies, to my error of having too high expectations, to my fear that people would mock me, to my inability to see the small successes I already had, to how I had allowed everyone to have an opinion over my life, and so on. She made me realize that I owed no one an explanation. I was able to get rid of the fear of the unknown. My confidence was rekindled, and then my soaring high began tremendously.

Gradually, I rediscovered my passion for business, teaching, and education.

Today, I am fulfilled and happy again. Jesus took care of me and kept His promise. Today, I am incredibly grateful to God.

Now, I am not only an achiever (a Child Psychologist) but also an advocate for children who may be stigmatized and left behind academically due to a disability, learning difficulty, or any other cognitive issue. I advocate for Inclusive Education through my NGO. Through this work, many children are rescued, with better learning outcomes and a promising, happy life ahead of them.

Now I am living my best life happily and fulfilled, helping others along the way.

THANK YOU, JESUS!

About Olukemi Awodokun

A Child Psychologist with expertise in Special Needs Education and Inclusive Education, Olukemi Awodokun runs an NGO that caters to teacher training in schools for Inclusive Education and proper diagnoses and intervention for children with special needs. She is also involved in public enlightenment campaigns on Inclusive Education through her social media handles and intends to extend her advocacy reach through mass media soon.

Email: theheadstartscholarfoundation@gmail.com

3

Journey of Learning about Depression

By *Jimmy Tan San Tek*

My journey with Depression

My first memory of experiencing depression is probably when I was growing up as a shy, nerdy teenager trying to fit in during my secondary school days.

At that young age, during my formative years, finding a sense of identity and belonging was important to me. There were days when I felt depressed and left out.

The sense of loneliness persisted when I joined the outdoor activities club in junior college. I was teased and called derogatory names for being introverted and not conforming to the norms of a typical outgoing, talkative youth.

After serving national service and entering university, I reached a point where I felt rejected, depressed, and even suicidal. Life seemed directionless and meaningless as I grappled with an existential crisis.

Reading self-help books and attending religious services in churches only provided temporary relief from bouts of depression. However, I still struggled with depression from time to time.

A Fresh Look at Depression

In recent years, it has occurred to me that depression could be seen from a different perspective. As the word implies, "depression" refers to something that is pressed down or suppressed.

So, if we visualize depression as a physical entity, we can see it represented as a hollow in the ground. On land, depression may resemble a valley, and in the ocean, it may take the form of a trench. Speaking of which, the deepest part of the Earth's surface is nearly 11,000 m deep at the Mariana Trench in the Pacific Ocean.

Interestingly, our bodies are similar to the Earth's surface, composed of about 70% water and 30% solid matter. Just as depressions are inherent to the planet, they are also inherent to our humanity.

This implies that we cannot simply wish away or completely eliminate depression because life is meant to be experienced as a cycle. There are highs and lows in our lives, much like there are mountains and valleys, or continents and trenches.

What I Learned About Dealing with Depression

One important lesson I learned about dealing with depression is that it is not about simply overpowering it with willpower or attempting to ignore it through busyness or distractions. It is also not about suppressing it with drugs, medication, or alcohol, nor about minimizing it through intellectual or spiritual bypassing.

Rather, we need to acknowledge depression, embrace it as a part of life, and allow ourselves to experience the difficult emotions that come with it. We should let these emotions pass through our bodies. We can acknowledge depression in its various forms, such as sadness, grief, sorrow, anxiety, moodiness, melancholy, trauma, or even suicidal tendencies.

As alarming as it may sound, depression doesn't actually kill us. It is how we respond to depression that determines whether we can overcome it. While depression can feel overwhelming, expressing our thoughts and feelings through writing or verbalizing them allows us to recognize that our worst imaginations often aren't as terrible as they had initially appeared in our minds.

This isn't to trivialize depression or suggest that it's merely a figment of the imagination. Instead, it emphasizes the importance of recognizing and understanding depression by validating our emotions and expressing them in ways that feel comfortable to us. This can be through art, music, poetry, journaling, or any other form of self-expression.

In a sense, depression feels intensely personal because only we ourselves know precisely how we feel in a particular situation. As a wise man once wrote, "No one else can truly know how sad or happy you are" (Proverbs 14:10, CEV).

On the other hand, we are not alone in experiencing depression because many people have felt the same way as us in similar situations. This realization becomes evident when reading this collection of real-life stories.

Another way of dealing with depression that I learned is through prayer. Prayer involves communing with a higher power that we believe in, whether we refer to it as God, our highest self, the Universe, the Great Spirit, a guardian angel, or any other term we resonate with.

Alternatively, we can choose to take a walk in nature, as studies have shown that being surrounded by greenery or water and breathing in fresh air can uplift our spirits. The melodic sounds of bird songs or the soothing presence of certain charismatic animals, such as pet dogs and dolphins, can also have a positive impact on our mood.

I am grateful that by practicing these natural remedies instead of relying on pharmaceutical drugs, I have been able to effectively manage depression whenever it resurfaces, especially in relation to early life trauma.

If you are reading my story and have also experienced depression, I hope that it provides some form of assistance or guidance.

About Jimmy Tan San Tek

Jimmy Tan San Tek is a nonconformist writer, editor, editorial trainer, photographer, videographer and digital music artist. He provides editorial services to help people write better English so that they can express themselves more clearly to their intended audience. He also advocates for nature conservation and environmental sustainability. For more information, please check out his website at https://jimmytst.wordpress.com

4

A Journey Into Health & Happiness

By Jessica See

"Health is not just an absence of disease. It's an inner joyfulness that should be ours all the time, a state of positive well-being." - *Deepak Chopra*

When I was in my second year at the National University of Singapore, I suffered from chronic insomnia and depression. I was away from my home and family in Kuala Lumpur, stressed out from studies on subjects I had absolutely no interest in, and to top it all off – blaming myself for a relationship breakup. I was seeing a psychiatrist, and prescribed various anti-depressants and sleeping pills – which grew stronger and more potent as time passed, yet my condition did not seem to improve.

My health deteriorated as well – I had severe migraines, gastric pains, irritable bowel syndrome, you name it. I was staying at the then Nanyang Campus hostel. I remember I had to sleep with a small pail beside my bed, as I would be constantly throwing up. In short, I was a mess.

What woke me up – literally – was a dream I had while I was living with a few university mates in a rented HDB apartment in Jurong East. It was our final year, and we had moved out from the hostel. The dream was so real, I'm not even sure if it was a dream or not.

One morning, after finally being knocked out from a sleeping pill, I was in the netherworld of sleep, where the dreaming brain creates an entire world of its own. In my dream (was it a dream?) I saw myself getting up, walking to the window in the kitchen, at the back of the apartment, and… jumping down.

I woke up in shock. It was so real, I was trembling with fear.

From that moment on, I made a decision not to take any more of the pills.

But it was a long road to regain my health. After graduation, I started working at a clock watching job at a finance company in Singapore, which didn't help at all. For the three years I worked there as a credit officer, I was like a zombie – I did not have any real purpose except to wait for time to pass. I was constantly sick and on medical leave at least once a fortnight.

The moment my mandatory three years was up – I was on a student loan, which meant I had to work in Singapore for at least three years, I packed up my bags, and returned to my home country of Malaysia.

Together with some partners, I started a publishing company and launched a business magazine for women. Well, as you can guess, all my physical and mental troubles fled. The cure? My passion for what I was engaged in. I couldn't afford to pay myself very much, but it was such a joy to have a clear focus on what I wanted to achieve with my magazine! It was one of the best nine years of my life – new endeavors, great adventures, lots of learning as I had zero knowledge of the publishing world at that time – all fueled by passion for a clear mission bigger than myself.

Certainly, as Plato once observed, the cure of the part should not be attempted without the treatment of the whole. No attempt should be made to cure the body without the soul. And if the heart and body are to be healthy, you must begin by curing the mind. In other words, we all need to be healed in the highest sense by making ourselves perfect in mind, body and spirit, and says Dr. Chopra in his book, Journey into Healing, the first step is to realise that this is even possible.

"To have a renewed body, you must be willing to have new perceptions that give rise to new solutions," explains Dr. Chopra. "If you look closely at your own life, you will realise that you are sending signals to your body that repeat the same old fears and wishes, the same old habits of yesterday and the day before. That is why you are stuck with the same old body."

So if we are getting sick or feeling depressed all the time, we have to recognise that our bodies are telling us that something is not right, either spiritually or mentally, as well as physically. We cannot simply ignore the signals and hope they'll go away with a dose or two of antibiotics, or whatever other medication.

A note on taking sleeping pills or even alcohol to help us sleep: these do not help us sleep, they simply serve to knock us out. Being knocked out is not sleep. I must thank my health coach who specialize in sleep medicine for this great insight, Dr Chen Ye Hong. Now I know why I was like a zombie in those days – despite the hours of "sleep" I got after downing some pills, it was not the good quality deep sleep or REM sleep that my body needed. That was why I woke up tired each day, instead of being fresh and ready to take on the world.

So now I know, we can't argue with our body on what it needs. We can't deny the stress we put it through with sleep deprivation or following unhealthy habits like smoking, or excessive drinking, for instance. It's no use pushing reality aside. Because sooner or later, it catches up with us and by that time, no amount of regret or remorse can alleviate the suffering, not only our own but also of our family and friends, when we get really sick.

Dr. Chopra feels that bad habits are just the "worn-out ruts of the mind, paths that once led to freedom because they opened up new thoughts, but now lead nowhere." His observation that "my tormentor is myself left over from yesterday" should motivate all of us to put our past habits behind us and start anew.

So where do we start? First and foremost by loving ourselves. Have respect for ourselves – our capabilities, intelligence, recognising our good qualities – and for our bodies. Then we have to feed our spirit, mind and body with proper, nutritious diets, and not putting poison in.

Like not watching or reading or eating for that matter, TRASH. (No more chasing soap operas that make you cry and cry. And you wonder why you feel so sad most of the time!) Like going for regular rejuvenating and stress-free holidays, with lots of fresh air and sunlight. Naturopaths even recommend air baths which basically involves wandering about without any clothes on for a few minutes, so that your skin can breathe. Like fasting or going on a fruit or vegetable diet for short periods to cleanse the system.

For me, how I "cured my insomnia" was to simply get into the sun! Now, when I wake up in the morning, I will go outside my apartment onto the corridor, and simply soak up the early morning sun while I do my deep breathing exercises. In the evening, I enjoy the evening sun when the sun sets, either in a nearby park or at home. This allows my master clock to reset my circadian rhythm. And when it's time to go to bed, I go to bed. If I'm not sleepy yet, I just lie in bed, read a novel for a while and finally, do some progressive muscle relaxation.

I also make sure I take healthy foods so my body gets the nutrients it needs e.g. foods rich in tryptophan, a sleep-promoting substance. I avoid taking caffeine in the afternoon; only one coffee in the morning for me.

As Dr. Chopra admonishes, "Attend to your own inner health and well-being. Allow your love to nourish yourself as well as others. Do not strain after the needs of life…. Life is here to enjoy."

And of course, most importantly, to understand why I feel the way I do. One thing that I learnt as I went on my journey towards health and happiness – to understand my own feelings and unmet needs better. When I was getting my certification for Neuro-Linguistic Programming, and going through a process called timeline therapy, I discovered I had a deep-seated feeling of guilt that was encompassing my life. The most amazing part was, I managed to trace it back to when I was in my mother's womb!

At the time that my mother was pregnant with me, my family had just downgraded from a big house to a small two-bedroom apartment. My father was addicted to gambling and heavily in debt. So my poor pregnant mother would sit by the window waiting for my father to come back, and crying. From the timeline therapy, I was brought back right into my mother's womb, curled up like a foetus, feeling the guilt of my mother's pain! I could feel her misery, and feel guilty that somehow, I was the one who brought it on. This was further enforced by stories I hear later – how life was so good for the family before I was born….

So that led to decades of self-blame for myself. The most vivid recollection I have of feeling guilty was when I got my O' Level results. I had scored A's in every subject I took, and yet instead of feeling happy, it only served to put me in a state of depression as I felt I didn't deserve them. It was crazy! My mother took one look at my face when I returned home with my results, and thought I had failed in the exams!

That feeling followed me through my university days, life in the workplace and even when I first started my magazine. I would beat myself up for every mistake that I overlooked. I went through countless sleepless nights wishing very hard that I could turn back the clock and live life differently.

It was the timeline therapy that helped me to realise what the root cause of my feelings of guilt was, and to reframe what was in my subconscious mind. Of course, I was not to be blamed for the financial troubles of my family. I learnt to stop taking the blame for every negative situation in my life, and instead to acknowledge that it has happened and to always ask myself, "What do I learn from this?" This way, I turn every negative experience or what some people call "failure" into a lesson, and to go into the future, bearing the wisdom of my regrets. I learnt to forgive myself, and be self-compassionate.

Last, but certainly not least, through it all, I had one powerful force on my side that never left me, even when I had forgotten all about Him – I'm talking about God, of course.

The lyrics of Lauren Daigle's song You Say ring in my mind even as I write this:

I keep fighting voices in my mind that say I'm not enough
Every single lie that tells me I will never measure up
Am I more than just the sum of every high and every low
Remind me once again just who I am because I need to know

You say I am loved when I can't feel a thing
You say I am strong when I think I am weak
And you say I am held when I am falling short
And when I don't belong, oh You say I am Yours
And I believe
Oh, I believe
What You say of me
I believe
The only thing that matters now is everything You
think of me
In You I find my worth, in You I find my identity

Often, we just need to have someone to believe in us, so we can believe in ourselves.

Being able to turn my own life around is what gives me such passion to help others as a health coach, and to multiply my efforts by training and equipping other people to do the same. My mission is to change the world, one person at a time. What is yours?

The world needs more people who can be compassionate, there to provide a listening ear and a helping hand. As actress Michelle Yeoh said at a recent Harvard Law School graduation keynote address, compassion is the ultimate superpower within us: "The prerequisite to change is empathy. Seeing through other people's perspectives activates our compassion, which becomes the driving force for real-world demonstrable action."

So, here's to a healthy lifestyle, and a healthy, happy life. And remember, the blueprint for perfect health is inside you.

About Jessica See

Jessica See is the founder of Health Coach International, and a pioneer in the area of health coaching in Asia. She has trained and certified more than 300 health coaches, many of whom work in the area of mental health coaching. She is also the editor for Mind Matters, a magazine published by Over the Rainbow, a one-stop hub for youth mental wellness in Singapore. You can find out more about her work at www.healthcoachesasia.com

5

My Story of Depression

By Tamikio Dooley

I want to share my story of how I cope with depression. My name is Tamikio Dooley. My doctor diagnosed me with depression at sixteen-years-old. Today, I'm forty-eight-years-old. Aside from five sexual assaults, three attempted and two sexual assaults, I've been through emotional, verbal, psychological, and financial maltreatment. During depression, I was overcome with grief, fatigue, dejection, insomnia, and sobbed over anything. Instead of losing interest in eating, I would overeat. I became disheartened over past struggles with assaults. Being thin, no matter how much I gorged, the emotional, verbal, psychological, and financial mistreatment had its effect more since I had to confront it routinely. I had no energy or interest hanging around family and friends, or going places doing the things I enjoyed most of the time. I was nervous and cranky, but honestly, I never thought about death or tried committing suicide, but buried my unhappiness, concealing my inner pain.

Meandering through life suffering from emotional pain more than physical pain, yet the sexual assaults were enough, causing tremendous physical pain. I attempt to leave the past aggressions in the past, but there was still the emotional abuse, hovering in my head in shadowy places. Feeling oppressed, like I could not breathe, because I had that monkey on my back. Confused, solitary, even though my life was bordered by family, friends, and acquaintances, but I kept my depression confidential from the world. There are other dreadful events and things associated with my depressed moments, but I prefer not sharing the drastic just yet. I continue suffering with depression today, but learning how to handle its ramifications.

When first diagnosed with depression, my doctor prescribed antidepressants to treat my major depressive disorder. I experienced anxiety disorders, and addicted to multiple medications such as painkillers, sleeping aids to help me sleep, and alcohol sometimes.

Apart from that, I would like to share some steps I took coping with depression. I continue to take some of these steps of coping today. Depression ambushed me last week like in my teenage and mid-life years. I grapple with depression but with limits. I stay active, but not as regularly as I should. My dietary habits are under control some days consuming healthy foods. I established appropriate hours for sleep at night. Every single day, I find an additional reason for living. I concentrate on friends, family, and associates sharing similar interests, such as writing, reading, networking, social events, and other activities uniting people. I formulate a list of small goals to achieve and accomplished most of them, documenting a personal journal recording my thoughts each week. When the week draws to a close, I go back and read my journal. This reminiscence clears my mind. I set aside some time once a week listening and dancing to music. A good movie directs my negative feelings to positive depending on the movie. I've even concocted a creative flow, expressing positive emotions, no longer isolating myself from the world and get out into the world, surrounding myself with people who enjoy similar activities, recognizing, and appreciate my surroundings, choosing carefully the people I want to be around. I practice mindfulness for calming and soothing, investigating more meditation apps. The thing I enjoy doing is collecting candle warmers and candles, especially aromatherapy candles, setting the tranquil atmosphere. Believe it or not, these tips help to cope with depression. While depression is long-term and sometimes life threatening, it never goes away. Through spiritual guidance, I seek the prayerful life and God for strength. I'm a firm believer in God.

We just have to discover how to cope with depression in our separate ways.

It's a continual, lifelong process.

When I become inundated through depression, I know it doesn't just go away. I don't hesitate administering some of the steps and tips, or talking to a close friend, family member, or someone with expert credentials for help.

Love and support are a huge dose of coping.

About Tamikio L. Dooley

Tamikio L. Dooley is a multi award-winning author. She writes nonfiction, poetry, short stories, essays, articles, and inspiring books.

Tamikio received the World Literary Award 2022, International Peace Medal Award, Peace Award, the Woman Leader in Transcendence Award, won her first crystal trophy award, and other awards.

She is the author of Inspire Me to Heal, Relationship Boundaries, and The Power of Business.

Website: https://www.dooleysbooks.com/

6

Embracing the Sunlight Within

By Faranaz Mahmood Khan

Nadine, a close friend of mine, is a 45-year-old woman who's remarkably gritty and courageous. She frequently confronts life head-on, never backing down, even when the going gets tough. I often find myself admiring her, perplexed at how she remains serene amidst the storm of life's trials, as they continuously barrage her. Here unfolds her inspiring story.

A few months into her marriage with her cherished fiancé, Kay, Nadine discovered she was pregnant. Both Kay and Nadine were ecstatic as they had been eager to start a family. Their fondness for children made the prospect of having one of their own an absolute blessing. The arrival of their son Forrest, with his dark, upright hair, delicate features, and rosy skin, left everyone breathless. Kay and Nadine couldn't have been happier. It felt as if their family was now complete. Forrest brought immeasurable joy and happiness into their lives. As a mother,

Nadine learned to prioritize Forrest's needs and those of her family above her own.

Ten months after that joyous occasion, Nadine was at work when she received a distressing call from Kay. Sobbing uncontrollably on the phone, Kay shared some dreadful news. He was at the hospital for a persistent stomach pain when the doctors discovered a malignant tumor on his pancreas. Nadine felt as if her world was collapsing. The harmonious bubble she had carefully crafted with her family was suddenly shattered. The future, once bright and promising, now appeared bleak as Kay and Nadine struggled to navigate their day-to-day lives. Despite working closely with the medical team, Kay's condition worsened, and there was little sign of improvement.

Regrettably, the tumor was aggressive and inoperable due to its location on a vital organ. Kay underwent countless sessions of radiotherapy and chemotherapy, which weakened him considerably, yet the tumor remained, stubborn as an old oak root deeply entrenched in the ground and refusing to budge. Over the next few years, the doctors could only attempt to control the tumor's growth as Kay, thankfully, continued to stay active, albeit frequently plagued with pain and discomfort. Meanwhile, my once vibrant friend Nadine became quiet, withdrawing from her social life. She ceased attending social events, choosing instead to isolate herself. Numerous attempts to contact her were in vain. It seemed she had lost interest in her hobbies and any social interaction. When I finally managed to speak with her, she confided that life had drastically changed for her and Kay.

Nadine could no longer be the carefree individual she once was. Her every waking moment was consumed with worry and stress, as Kay's condition more or less remained static. He required constant medication, without which he would feel unwell for days. They had exhausted all their savings and were now reliant on the support of others, especially since Kay lacked medical insurance. Nadine completely lost interest in advancing her career; she fulfilled her work obligations out of necessity, needing to devote her primary focus to Forrest, who was blossoming beautifully, and Kay, who remained ill. Nadine mostly felt a sense of hopelessness, as there was little she could do to help Kay besides praying for his recovery and providing physical support.

Although Nadine never labeled herself as such—a fact for which I was immensely grateful—I could tell she was grappling with some form of depression. She was no longer the person she used to be. A few years later, Kay's tumor became cancerous, introducing further challenges into Nadine's life and that of her family. Nadine never stopped supporting Kay, even if it meant sacrificing her own happiness and comfort. She considered herself fortunate that Kay, for the most part, retained his independence and could still work and move freely despite his illness. There were days when Kay would be incapacitated by pain, but he would rally for his family, continuing to work to cover the daily expenses and medical bills. Nadine drew quiet strength from Kay's resilience, finding comfort in the knowledge that her husband was still by her side, even in the face of potential collapse or death.

Nadine shared with me her belief that God had been kind to her and her family. Despite the hardships they endured, they had the privilege of living and remaining together all these years. Nadine is thankful that God has granted Kay a much longer life expectancy than initially predicted. She recalls the doctor telling Kay that he wouldn't live beyond a year—a time when Forrest was just one. Today, Forrest is sixteen and Kay still battles cancer. Kay's cancerous pancreatic tumor was recently removed due to successful shrinkage. Though this is encouraging news, Nadine confided that the cancer has spread to his lungs and possibly his head as well. Kay needs to continue receiving weekly medication if he is to maintain a decent quality of life; otherwise, his condition may deteriorate rapidly.

Each time I receive updates from Nadine, I am amazed and inspired by how she navigates the trials with her family, maintaining her wit and bravery. Nadine shared that, despite enduring bleak episodes in her life, she chooses to stand tall and strong, confident in the belief that God is with them at all times. Only close family members were privy to Kay's health condition because he opted to keep it private due to his reserved nature. Nadine often feels judged by others for her absence at annual family gatherings and occasional weddings. People perceive her and her husband as arrogant and antisocial. However, due to the sensitive nature of Kay's condition, she allows these misconceptions to persist out of respect for Kay's decision to keep his illness confidential.

Is Kay still sick today?
Yes.
Will Kay eventually get better or recover fully?
No one knows.
Are there days when Nadine feels like giving up and letting go?
She confessed that there are.
She admitted there have been times when the burden feels too heavy to bear, and she's been tempted to run away from it all.

However, Nadine remains strong to this day. She combats the depressive episodes in her life by engaging in activities she enjoys and taking long walks to destress. Having Forrest by her side brightens her days significantly. He has matured into a wonderful young man who shares a close bond with his mother.

As a dear friend, I continually pray for sunlight to break through the stormy clouds in Nadine's life once and for all. I am perpetually inspired by Nadine's resilience in the face of the persistent pain and sadness she endures.

I have faith and pray that one day, Nadine will regain her radiant smile. That she will once again embrace the sunlight within her.

About Faranaz Mahmood Khan

A connoisseur of the finer things in life, Faranaz enjoys English literature, exquisite poetry, and theater. Whether she's traveling overseas or just taking a break, she prefers beach walks, countryside strolls, and mountain treks. As an educator by profession, she embodies and instills values of kindness and compassion in the children she encounters. With a wild heart and a mind full of daydreams, she thrives in the ideals she cultivates within her imagination. On carefree days, she indulges in writing, cooking, reading, and cycling, along with learning new things, such as baking gluten-free or sourdough bread. She has also lent her skills to friends as an editor and copywriter.

https://www.instagram.com/nat_fara/

https://www.facebook.com/natdia.faranaz

7

Highly Functional Depression

By Lee Li Li

I have always harbored these feelings inside me: low self-esteem, unworthiness, hopelessness, constant sadness, difficulty experiencing joy, fatigue, and an inability to relax and slow down my thoughts, even to the extent of contemplating being better off dead, and the list goes on.

When I feel this way, I tend to avoid social activities and feel reluctant to engage in them. I struggle to maintain healthy relationships, suffer from insomnia or oversleep to escape the mental turmoil, and find it challenging to get out of bed. Countless nights, I cry myself to sleep, even entertaining thoughts of suicide as a means to end the emotional pain.

However, at the same time, I have been able to maintain my day-to-day functioning. I've fulfilled all my responsibilities, such as studying, going to work, and performing well. I also manage to keep the house organized and clean, meet both family and work expectations, and occasionally engage in social activities.

I've been wondering what is wrong with me. From the outside, I appear fine and function normally, but internally, I am struggling and crying out for help in my seemingly meaningless life. It frustrates me that I can't experience joy, and my low mood often leads those close to me to perceive a distance when all I truly desire is a sense of belonging and connection. I long to laugh happily with my child, but even his efforts to make me laugh only bring about my own frustration, leaving me awash in guilt. I wish I could be as carefree and silly as him, but for some reason, I just can't.

Going on holidays feels like a waste of time and money, as I can't seem to find any difference or joy in those experiences. When I'm feeling down, my entire life seems to come to a halt. I stop doing anything and escape into sleep until my head becomes heavy and painful, or until it's time for me to fulfill my responsibilities.

Alternatively, I indulge in binge-watching dramas to avoid the chaos within my mind. If my son catches me watching a movie, he recognizes that I'm feeling miserable and maintains his distance. My life becomes stagnant until I'm forced to confront reality once again. Hours, days, months, and even years of my life are spent in a futile attempt to escape from the truth.

I have so many dreams and passions, so many things I want to do, but I can't muster the strength to pursue them because I constantly doubt myself. I frequently wonder how much longer I can endure before I finally succumb to the desire to end my life and escape this emotional pain.

When I was younger, I resisted thoughts of suicide because I worried that there would be no one to take care of my mother, who had struggled throughout her whole life. Now that I have my own child, I resist those thoughts each time they arise, fully aware that my son's well-being would be affected if I were no longer around. I'm concerned that there doesn't seem to be anyone I trust or believe is capable of understanding and managing his unique mindset.

I want to leave without regrets, which has prompted me to secure insurance plans and execute a will. This way, my family members will have quicker financial access to sustain themselves when I'm no longer around. I have even purchased a columbarium space and pre-planned my funeral arrangements, ensuring that my family won't be left in a difficult situation. I'm preparing everything I can while my mind is still functioning well because I know that someday, when the emotional pain becomes unbearable, I may not be able to resist thoughts of suicide.

Sometime in my mid-20s, during an office lunch break, I stumbled upon an article in The Star newspaper about depression and the available treatment at Universiti Hospital, a government hospital located in the city center not too far from where I live. It was like a revelation when I realized there was a name for what I had been experiencing all along: 'Depression'! The article perfectly described the feelings I had been grappling with - the inability to find joy in life, overwhelming sadness, excessive guilt, hopelessness, mood swings, and so much more. Discovering that others also struggled with similar mental battles was a tremendous relief. I began to realize that I wasn't 'crazy' or abnormal, as I had always believed.

Carrying the hope that I could receive treatment and finally alleviate the internal struggles in my mind, I went through the hassle of securing an appointment at the government hospital. After enduring a half-day wait, I was disappointed to find out that I would only be seeing a Medical Officer for a brief consultation of less than 30 minutes, instead of the specific professor mentioned in the newspaper article. I was prescribed Prozac, an antidepressant. I held onto the belief that this medication would alleviate my melancholy and allow me to find enjoyment in the activities I once loved. With patience, I waited for the remaining half of the day at the pharmacy to collect my prescribed medicine, which was provided free of charge.

To my surprise, I noticed a decrease in agitation towards others at work, and my mood improved throughout the day when I started taking the antidepressant. However, as the effects of the medication wore off in the evening, I experienced a profound sense of despair, feeling incredibly low and becoming easily irritated by even the smallest things. To escape this overwhelming feeling, all I could do was force myself to sleep as soon as I returned from work until the following morning. There were even instances where I would spend the entire weekend in bed, sleeping from Friday night until Sunday night.

After enduring these emotional ups and downs for about six months, I made the decision to no longer rely solely on medication and instead began searching for the underlying cause of my depression. Another factor that motivated me to explore alternatives was the limited amount of annual leave I had available, which made it challenging to visit the hospital on a monthly basis.

Since my teenage years, I have dedicated a significant amount of time to browsing through libraries and bookstores, reading self-help and motivational books in an attempt to uplift my mood and cope with the internal struggles I face. I yearn to be like those who can genuinely laugh and experience true happiness, rather than merely putting on a smile. I long to live my life without constantly pondering the purpose of it all.

Despite being alive, I feel like a person devoid of vitality. I vividly recall my secondary school counselor using a Malay proverb, 'hidup segan, mati tak mau' (roughly translated as 'too timid to live, but unwilling to die'), which perfectly encapsulates the essence of my existence.

I came to the realization that I had been relying on others for my happiness and self-esteem. When I no longer received validation or support from my partner, friends, or family members, the resulting stress and frustration would trigger my depression once again. Even a simple remark or criticism about not being good enough would lead me to believe that I would be better off dead. Prior to my marriage, I would constantly change partners, hoping that love and care would uplift my mood. However, this cycle persisted, with episodes of depression being triggered time and time again.

Over the years, I sought help from private practitioners as well, but none of the psychiatrists I saw were able to alleviate the intense feelings I experienced. Unfortunately, due to my limited income, I couldn't afford frequent monthly or bi-weekly follow-up consultations, so I continued to struggle on my own.

On many occasions, the pain inside me and the conflicting thoughts in my mind led me towards thoughts of suicide as a way to end the suffering.

During my younger days, every morning while commuting in reckless minibusses, I purposely chose the front seat (for higher risk) and desperately wished for an accident to occur, hoping it would bring an end to my life and the pain I felt.

Later on in life, when I started driving, there were moments when words from my son or husband, or certain actions from them, would trigger such intense emotions that I would find myself wishing I could just crash into something and escape through death.

However, the ironic part was that I never wanted other road users to be injured or become victims of my actions. This internal conflict only added to my misery, questioning why I had to consider so many factors just to put an end to my mental pain. It fueled a strong sense of self-hatred and led me to seek solace in self-pity. Many tearful nights filled with sorrow became a part of my journey as a parent.

I faced challenging times raising my differently wired son, starting from the time he was just a fetus. His unique sleep patterns kept me awake during the night until the early morning, depriving me of much-needed rest. Despite having a demanding job in the corporate world, I was fortunate to have an understanding employer who granted me flexibility in my work hours.

From my son's constant need for attachment since birth to his defiant behavior as he grew older, along with the phone calls and meetings with school authorities regarding his performance and discipline issues, as well as conflicts with my spouse over our differing parenting approaches, and the pressure from other family members, I felt overwhelmingly burdened. These circumstances often led me into periods of depression. When I would gaze at my son while he slept, I felt an immense sense of guilt for the hardships I caused him, realizing that I couldn't be the supportive and cheerful mother he needed. I constantly apologized and vowed to control my mood, but as the hectic days unfolded, juggling work, house chores, and family responsibilities, I found myself spiraling out of control once again.

I would say that a significant portion of my financial resources has been dedicated to seeking help from doctors, therapists, and attending various courses. However, my family members viewed these actions as unnecessary and believed that I was simply wasting money due to my "overthinking" problem. It became evident that none of them truly understood what I was going through and the profound impact that depression was having on me. Despite enduring decades of mental torment, it feels like a miracle that I have managed to survive.

Finally, two years ago, I experienced a breakthrough after silently suffering for the past 40 years. It was a combination of consultations with psychiatrists, psychotherapy, health coaching, and the support of compassionate individuals I met that brought about a transformation in my life. While seeking help for my teenage son's depression, we discovered that, apart from his educational challenges, a major cause of his stress leading to depression was actually me—due to my tendencies as a perfectionistic parent.

I was advised to learn to let go of my expectations for my son, which prompted me to seek further consultations with psychotherapists and psychiatrists for myself. I realized that I was experiencing high levels of stress due to my pursuit of perfection, being overly protective, and constantly battling with myself over how to be a good parent. Throughout this time, the focus had always been on therapy and consultations for my son's challenges, with no assistance offered to help me cope with my own struggles as a vulnerable parent.

During the private psychiatrist consultations, I received the diagnosis that I had been suffering from a condition known as Persistent Depressive Disorder. It was a shocking revelation for me to realize that I had actually been experiencing depression since as early as 9 years old.

Looking back on my childhood, as far as I can recall from the age of 5, I struggled to connect with other children and didn't find as much enjoyment in playtime as my siblings and neighbors did. I found it difficult to experience joy, and I often believed that I was too shy or simply unable to socialize properly.

Starting at the age of 9, I began daydreaming about running away from home or contemplating ways to end my life because I felt incredibly out of place and as if nobody cared about me, even though I had four siblings to play with.

I also came across the term 'high-functioning depression,' which accurately describes my condition. Despite the internal mental struggles, I have managed to maintain functionality and perform well in my work. This prompted me to engage in extensive reading on mental health to gain knowledge and reflect on my own experiences.

I am incredibly grateful to have been assigned a psychotherapist, Dr. Sujata, who has helped me gain a better understanding of myself. Through our sessions, we delved into the concept of intergenerational trauma, exploring the traumas that both my spouse and I experienced during our childhoods, which have influenced our behaviors and thought patterns. With this newfound understanding, I no longer blame myself or my spouse for what's not working in our family. I am able to fully accept myself for who I am and practice self-care and self-love. I've learned to communicate with my inner child when conflicting thoughts and actions arise.

In addition, I delved into the theory of 'conscious parenting' by Dr. Shefali Tsabary, the New York Times bestselling author of 'The Conscious Parent.' This newfound knowledge has empowered me to improve my communication skills and strengthen the bond with my son.

As a result of these changes within myself, my son has also experienced a faster recovery from his depression. I am grateful for the progress we have made together on this journey of healing and growth. Additionally, the Taoist parable 'Who knows what is good and what is bad' has enlightened me and allowed me to let go of my need for control. In the past, when things didn't turn out the way I wanted them to, especially with my son, I would become frustrated and depressed, worrying about the potential negative effects.

At the same time, I made the decision to pursue a health coaching course to equip myself with the necessary tools to guide my way out of depression. I wanted to become self-reliant and reduce the financial burden of monthly psychiatrist bills and expensive antidepressant medications. Learning about the processes of coaching and therapy has empowered me to live life to the fullest. I have become highly productive, engaging in multiple projects such as writing this book and embarking on my journey as a health coach.

I am immensely grateful to my master trainer in health coaching, Jessica See, and my fitness coach, Eve Tan Pei Yi, for their unwavering guidance and humble support. Through their mentorship, I have experienced a significant shift in how I utilize my time, no longer wasting it on movies or oversleeping. Instead, I am eager to apply my certified health coaching skills and extensive knowledge of nutrition to assist others in living a sustainable and healthier lifestyle. I am excited about the opportunity to make a positive impact on the lives of others.

I am now equipped with the skills to recognize negative patterns in my thoughts and behaviors. I have learned to change my mental blocks by shifting my perspective. Through self-analysis of my thinking patterns, I strive to adopt a positive and forward-thinking mindset. I have let go of the feelings of guilt and worry that used to weigh me down, no longer dwelling on the past or constantly fretting about the future.

Over the past two years, my life has undergone a holistic transformation as I achieved clarity of mind. I have accomplished significant weight loss, transitioning from obesity to reaching my ideal weight. Embracing a healthy diet through clean eating practices has positively impacted my overall well-being. Consistent exercise has become a regular part of my routine, benefiting both my physical and mental health. Perhaps most importantly, I have made significant progress in managing my stress, a crucial aspect of my journey towards wellness.

I no longer fear socializing and have overcome the belief that I cannot experience the joy of life. I feel blessed that my personal journey through depression, from darkness to light, has now become an opportunity for me to support and guide others in their own struggles. I believe that enduring these mental challenges was part of God's plan for me, as they have shaped me into a more insightful and compassionate person. My constant questioning of why I had to go through such torturous times has finally been answered. My purpose now is to help others live healthier lives, both physically and mentally. I firmly believe that everything happens for a reason, and this belief has given me strength and purpose throughout my journey.

I attribute my success to my determination and refusal to give up, taking the initiative to seek help. It's crucial for everyone to understand that reaching out for assistance is a significant step towards healing. However, the journey doesn't end there. The other half of the battle involves ongoing self-care and support because depression can persistently try to deceive you with negative and false thoughts such as 'You're worthless,' 'You're no good,' or 'No one cares.

If you need support in managing your depression or making healthier lifestyle choices, please don't hesitate to reach out to me. I'm here to offer guidance, support, and assistance.

About Lee Li Li

Lee Li Li is a certified health coach and parent. You can connect with her on Facebook at https://www.facebook.com/lee.li.587268 and on Instagram at:

https://www.instagram.com/lee.li.587268.

8

The Cries Within

By Hadi Al Maatiin

Depression is a common mental health disorder that affects millions of people worldwide. It can be a debilitating condition, causing a range of symptoms such as grief, sadness, hopelessness, and in some cases, fear. Mild depression is a type of depressive disorder that is characterized by persistent feelings of sadness, hopelessness, and low mood. These feelings may interfere with daily activities but are not severe enough to disrupt a person's life. Depression has a tremendous impact on an individual's life, and it can affect anyone, regardless of demographics such as age, gender, race, or background. However, depression can be treated. With the right support and treatment, those who are affected can successfully manage their symptoms and lead a fulfilling life.

I suffered from mild depression during my younger years. As I began writing this article, I found myself journeying back to a painful and sad phase of my life, to moments that almost broke me. My encounter with mild depression occurred during the aftermath of my first breakup. It was the first time I had fallen in love, and subsequently, the first time I had felt heartbreak. It was the initial experience I had with the agonizing pain of a severed relationship. The sensation was throbbing, as though my heart was being stabbed and punctured.

I was a naive teenager back then. At eighteen, I was still immature and brash. I had just dropped out of ITE and was working part-time at a café and a fast-food outlet. I was a carefree guy until the day I met a girl, who was fifteen, through the mIRC chat platform. This encounter would change the perspective of my life. We chatted for about a month or two before we decided to meet in person.

We decided to meet at Orchard Road and watch a movie. As I was preparing for this "blind date", the adrenaline rush was somewhat overwhelming because I had never seen her before, nor had we exchanged any pictures. We only exchanged contact numbers after three to four weeks of chatting. We spoke over the phone several times, especially during the weekends, as she was still in school. We described to each other what we would be wearing and tried to imagine what we might look like. As I approached the meeting spot with this "mysterious" girl, I felt butterflies in my stomach. I was nervous. I approached her and introduced myself.

She responded with a stunning smile. After the movie, we continued our conversation over dinner. All this time, I was quiet, simply observing her. I found myself merely smiling in response, perhaps captivated by her charisma. Suddenly, it was almost ten. She asked if I could take her home, and I obliged. Before parting ways, we promised to meet again the following week.

As I walked towards the train station, I found myself grinning from ear to ear. My heart was beating faster than before. I couldn't stop thinking about her; her smile had enraptured me. I felt as though I was on cloud nine. Was this true love? Had I really fallen in love for the first time? The feeling wasn't the same as the "puppy love" I had experienced before. This feeling was majestic. Fast forward a month, and we were officially boyfriend and girlfriend. I was ecstatic. I imagined that she might be the perfect girl whom I would marry in the future. She would be the one waiting for me every weekend when I returned from National Service, I thought. Our romance continued for nearly a year until she mentioned that her parents would like to meet me. Oh my God, I wasn't ready for this!

The day I met her parents was one I wished I hadn't experienced. Her mother, who was Malay, was accepting, but not her father. He hailed from an Arabic family lineage and was displeased at the prospect of having a non-Arab son-in-law. He expressed his dissatisfaction with me because I wasn't of Arab heritage. I was devastated. Since when has race become an issue in our modern society? He could simply have suggested that we refrain from meeting as frequently, given that she would be taking her 'O' Levels the following year. But why resort to the race card instead? I was at a loss for words. I couldn't process the situation. I left her place feeling disgusted and heartbroken. That night, I emailed her a short poem expressing my feelings for her, hoping to rekindle our relationship secretly. But she didn't reply. She also wasn't on our usual mIRC chat channel.

One day, I saw her and her family at the café where I worked. They didn't notice me in the corner, preparing their drink orders. She was holding hands with a young Malay man. Her father was enthusiastically conversing with him, who was paying for the orders. I then realized that this man was a young footballer, playing for a youth club in the S-League. My heart sank. I clenched my teeth, seething with anger. I held back my tears, not wanting to alarm my colleagues. She only noticed me when I was delivering their drinks. She didn't seem shocked at all, even introducing him to me excitedly. Her father then noticed me and made crude remarks about my job. I felt humiliated and embarrassed. I couldn't utter a word to defend myself. It felt as though my whole world was collapsing before my eyes. I just stood still, staring hard at them, clenching my fists in angst. I then walked away, leaving the café in sadness.

I was transported anew to this unpleasant moment. The humiliating words still echoed in my ears. Prior to this, I had lost my appetite and sleep. I didn't realize I was going through depression due to this broken relationship that had ended so poorly for me. Thereafter, I was not myself, especially after the incident. One night, I subconsciously slashed my arms. The excruciating pain was oddly thrilling. It seemed that when I bled, the internal pain would dissipate. I acted foolishly, hiding my scars with towels at home and wearing long-sleeved shirts when I went out.

In the following weeks, I worked every day, even taking on overtime, just to keep my mind occupied. My manager had noticed the episode from the previous week and saw how much I had changed. She had witnessed the entire drama. She saw my dejection and was worried about my well-being. After work one day, she approached me and we had a conversation over dinner. I kept denying my true emotions, suppressing my feelings. Physically, I appeared fine, but deep inside, I was falling apart. I couldn't let go of what had happened. I pretended to smile, merely to conceal the cries within.

"I'm sorry to hear that you're feeling this way. Please understand that it's common to experience feelings of sadness, hopelessness, and low energy at times. Don't suppress these emotions. I want you to know that I'm here for you."

I prayed fervently, hoping not to encounter my ex and her family again. A few months later, I was enlisted in National Service. At least I could attempt to erase the toxic memories that had been plaguing my life. As I matured, I realized how thoughtless and foolish I had been. If it hadn't been for my café manager speaking to me that day, I might have drowned in my own youthful sorrows and needless, self-inflicted stress. I am grateful that I didn't cause significant harm to myself, especially my mind. A mind once broken is difficult to mend.

Here are a few tips on how I recovered from depression naturally, without the use of any medicinal drugs:

1. Practice Self-Care: Attend to your basic needs such as getting enough sleep, eating healthy food, and exercising regularly. Maintaining good physical health has a positive impact on mental well-being.
2. Connect with Others: Reach out to family and friends or join a support group. Speak up. Talking to someone you trust can improve your mood and provide a sense of belonging and connection.

3. Practice Mindfulness: Spend a few minutes meditating, which can help you become more aware of your thoughts and emotions. Meditation also promotes compassion and self-acceptance.
4. Challenge Negative Thoughts: Shift your paradigm of thinking. When you notice you're being negative, challenge those thoughts and reframe them in a more positive light.

Remember, be gentle and patient with yourself as you navigate these feelings. Natural self-healing is a marathon, not a sprint. It takes years to improve, and a lifetime to maintain a healthy and positive mindset. Let me end this sharing with a poem:

"I am strong because I used to be weak.
I am perfect because I know my flaws.
I am fearless because I have been afraid.
I am wise because I have been foolish.
I can smile because I've known sadness.
I have a voice because I used to be voiceless.
My time as a caterpillar has expired.
It's time to spread my wings and fly.
Fly high, so high, that negativity is afraid to chase.
I will be the change I deserve to be.
I will be the change I want to see.
Every change starts with me, first.
I begin to live in the flow and true miracles start to happen."

About Hadi Al Maatiin

Hadi Al Maatiin has been a passionate writer since the age of fifteen, beginning with poems and articles in his native tongue. He later transitioned to writing in English. Despite a hectic work schedule, Hadi aspires to be a published author and continues to contribute high-quality articles and content. His ongoing writing project, "Tell A Story," has reached more than 500 days and can be found on his personal Facebook page. Visit and follow Hadi's work at:

https://www.facebook.com/profile.php?id=100063 9588845804&mibextid=ZbWKwL

9

The Optimistic Surface

By Anna Ng

To most of us, we tend to see people only at a surface level, and this extends to how we view ourselves as well.

To many, I come across as a very happy-go-lucky person, optimistic and positive. This perception spans from my secondary and polytechnic school friends, through my working life, and beyond.

As a real estate salesperson for more than a decade, I have always ensured that I appear neat, clean, and presentable, devoid of any off-putting odors that might affect anyone I come into contact with. As a result, I often receive compliments from clients, friends, and even strangers on my attire and, occasionally, my shoes.

In 2017, about a year after I joined ERA Realty Network Pte Ltd, I found my confidence and job satisfaction growing more than ever before. Sales were good, customers were loyal, and I felt truly invincible.

THE FALL

However, this was also the time that I encountered the strongest wave in the sea of life. An unfortunate incident involving me, my husband, and his family members left a deep impact on us.

I felt that they had committed an act so wrong, so unacceptable, that it profoundly breached my strict standards of morality and human rights.

When I raised the issue with my husband, I felt he was unsupportive. In fact, he questioned how my actions would impact his family later.

"Seriously?" I wondered. "At this point, you're still siding with your family, neglecting our own? Is this the man I thought I respected and married?" These questions circled my mind over and over.

THE CONFRONTATION

Like any other real estate agent facing ambiguity, I chose to confront his family about the matter.

However, it was my years of experience and skill as a salesperson that helped me realize, with startling clarity, that the family was not speaking the truth during our discussion. The confrontation did not go well; in fact, I ended up shouting at his family members and I nearly flipped the table.

To be frank, I had never been so infuriated in my life before.

I was severely incensed by my husband's reactions at the table, as well as by his family's responses. I could not comprehend their treatment of me. Why? On what grounds did I need to bow down to their preposterous attitudes?

THE DOWNWARD SPIRAL

Like a fast-paced, chaotic drama series, I found myself spiraling downward, quickly and uncontrollably. To ensure that all grievances were addressed, I chose to take significant action, including legal steps to ensure the wrongdoer was held accountable.

I had hoped that pursuing a legal resolution would bring me some form of closure to the matter that I was gripping onto so tightly. Instead, the issue dragged on for weeks and then months.

Closure eluded me.

Certainly, something could be done to make someone accountable for their wrongdoings.

Yet, I was so engrossed in my quest for revenge, in the name of seeking justice, that I unknowingly slipped into depression.

SELF-BLAME & NEVERENDING REGRET

Reflecting on the past, I am certain that I experienced a period of depression lasting 6-8 months. During this time, I reached a level of unhappiness where I began to regret many of my life decisions.

In the initial stages of those 6-8 months, I started to regret my marriage. I questioned why I had chosen to get married when my parents' own failed marriage served as evidence that it was a mistake. Divorce even crossed my mind as a possibility.

Furthermore, I began to regret willingly becoming pregnant, believing that my child was suffering as a result.

Lastly, I directed blame towards myself. As the one who brought my child into this world, I questioned why I had not protected her better from the start. I carried the weight of my parents' guilt, as if it were my own burden to bear.

THE ABYSS - CONTEMPLATING DEATH

During that period, I neglected my personal grooming and my work suffered as a result. I became a mere shell of myself, going through the motions of real estate activities like roadshows and prospecting, but with no fruitful outcomes. Negativity consumed me, and everything spiraled out of control.

In the depths of my self-reproach, I reached a point where I contemplated ending my own life. The pain of living became unbearable, and I felt utterly lost, unsure of how to rectify my circumstances or turn things around.

Fortunately, I lacked the courage to harm myself physically. However, every day, every waking moment of those 6-8 months, I prayed to God to take me away through death. Life seemed unbearably bitter, and I felt overwhelmed by regret and a sense of hopelessness.

God did not grant my wish for death; instead, I found myself waiting. As I waited for death to come, my half-lived existence persisted. During that struggle, I felt as though I had lost my usual touch in business, in life, and in my relationships with my family.

THE AWAKENING - SELF-REALIZATION THAT THINGS KEEP GOING WRONG

1. NO SALES

The first realization that something was amiss was when I noticed the absence of sales. No closings were happening, and I couldn't provide an answer to myself as to why.

2. WHAT IS CPD? I FORGOT...

The second realization that I was off track occurred when one of my associates asked if I had completed my CPD hours. I stared at her blankly and responded, "What CPD?" as if in a daze.

She was shocked by my response because no agent would ever forget about CPD. CEA guidelines required every sales agent in real estate to attend the necessary classes and fulfill a certain number of learning hours each year to maintain their skills.

3. CLIENT'S VIEWING SCHEDULE SCREWED UP

The third revelation came when I messed up my client's viewing schedule. This was a mistake I had never made since entering the trade in 2006. It was a clear sign that I had lost the attentiveness that is a fundamental requirement for a salesperson dealing with clients.

4. I FORGOT MY DAUGHTER'S NAME, BIRTHDATE, AND BIRTH CERTIFICATE NUMBER

The final shock to myself was realizing that I had completely forgotten my daughter's name, birthdate, and birth certificate number. How could I have let this happen?

I didn't have 20 daughters; I only have 2.

My world seemed to be crumbling before me, and I felt utterly helpless. Apart from work and family, I had nothing left. That moment of realization overwhelmed me.

I felt lost, experiencing this for the first time as an adult.

Despite all my prayers and pleas, God didn't take my life away. I started to wonder what other plans He had in store for me, as it seemed He wasn't ready to take back the flawed version of myself. At that time, I felt rather worthless.

THE TURNING POINT

My first turning point was nothing short of a miracle.

Miracles do happen, my friend, in both big and small ways in our daily lives. It just so happened that one of our female agents seemed to be facing even more issues than me. Our real estate leader asked me to invite her to his office at ERA for a discussion. He wanted to help.

I made the necessary arrangements, and he told me to come as well. However, at the last minute, she decided not to join us.

That day in my leader's office was a revelation. I hadn't anticipated sharing anything about my family problems, but I unexpectedly broke down in his office. I poured out to him everything that was going wrong with my sales and the challenges within my family.

He then began sharing his own personal story and recommended that I attend a course he believed would greatly benefit me. The course was held at Asia Works on Boon Tat Street.

TAKING ACTIONS TO BUY BACK MY SANITY

High on emotions, I decided to take his advice, signed the form through my teary eyes and paid a four figure sum for the course of a few days. It seemed expensive, but then i thought, how much would one put to buy back the sanity of myself???

I also thought, "Could he be scamming me? Maybe.." But I would rather go for a self improvement course than to go to the Buangkok mental institution for help. Frankly, even if I had gone to a mental asylum, who would know if I didn't tell anyone right?

But the stigma of it, recognising myself and labeling myself as a lunatic was too degrading to me. If i had done that, i felt i might have condemned myself beyond hope then.

I went for the course. Some people might call this the CBT Cognitive Behavioral Training.
It was a lot of help.
I mean, really.

SELF-AWARENESS & SELF-LOVE

The best gift I gave myself, as I reflect on the past, was the decision to invest my money and time in the CBT course. It was a commitment to my personal growth. Furthermore, I took another step by investing a five-figure sum to learn about online social media marketing.

As I reconsider the chain of events, I realize that despite the initial hardships, I have grown. I have grown from my former self who had never faced true adversity. I now understand that without the scars from past battles, one cannot be called a warrior.

I have grown from my previous belief that my identity was solely that of a real estate agent, nothing more. I have developed a deeper understanding of who I am.

I have become more accountable for myself, realizing that constantly blaming others and seeking revenge only kept me stuck in that moment. I have embraced the importance of sharing my own stories to inspire others.

I started questioning what I truly desired in life, and I found my answer.

Now, I am a podcaster sharing my stories in real estate, a co-author of three books, and a trainer for ERA agents, teaching them how to generate free leads through Facebook Live and storytelling for branding purposes. My aim is to add value to others' lives.

MY CONCLUSION

There is a common misconception that having depression equates to being mentally unsound or crazy. However, in my perspective, it is more of a mental illness that can be healed, just like any bodily illness. But in order to do so, we need to:

1. Acknowledge and realize that we need help.
2. Develop self-awareness of what has gone wrong, such as disruptions in daily activities or hobbies.
3. Specifically identify the areas in our lives that need improvement and change.
4. Take positive actions and make a commitment to prioritize self-love and self-healing. Over time, we can gradually recover and heal.

Depression should not be stigmatized or dismissed. It is an illness that requires understanding, support, and proactive steps towards recovery. By following these steps and showing self-compassion, we can gradually find our way back to a healthier and happier state of mind.

About Anna Ng
Anna is a happy-go-lucky individual, overcoming personal adversity from a troubled family background.

In 2018, amidst a successful real estate career that began in 2006, she encountered setbacks in her personal life that led to depression.

Now, in addition to her real estate work, she serves as a podcaster and a trainer at ERA. Anna aims to share her journey of overcoming depression through self-love and healing. Her mission is to inspire others to prioritize self-care and add value to their lives.

For more information, visit her website at www.clientcentricproperty.com.

10

Rising from the Shadows

By Carollyne Tong

Throughout my life, I have endured numerous crises that have brought me to my lowest points, but each time, I've managed to rebound with impressive speed. Now, I am convinced of my resilience and tenacity in all endeavours I undertake. If you're currently facing challenges or experiencing emotional turmoil, I sincerely hope that my personal journey can serve as a catalyst for your strength and instil in you the belief that you, too, can rise from the depths of despair to a life of triumph and enlightenment.

As a singer and songwriter myself, I hold great admiration for the late Coco Lee 李玟, who passed away on 5 July 2023. This chapter stands as a sincere and heartfelt tribute, profoundly affected by the news of her passing. Throughout my own musical journey, I often found myself singing her songs, captivated by her enchanting voice and captivating persona. I have a deep affection for her songs, especially "Before I Fall in Love," "被爱的女人 ," and "往日情."

DIVORCE

In 1999, I entered into marriage, but after seven years, my world was shattered when I discovered my spouse's infidelity. Consequently, I initiated divorce proceedings, and by early 2008, our marriage was legally dissolved. Custody of our six-year-old daughter was entrusted to me, and together, we sought refuge with my aging parents.

Navigating through the depths of despair, I felt an overwhelming darkness cast over me as I faced the responsibilities of raising my daughter. Alongside this emotional burden, I also contended with the loss of my job as a private piano teacher, which further intensified the challenges ahead. Under these heavy circumstances, my mental well-being greatly suffered. I found myself trapped in a relentless cycle of self-doubt. The belief that I was unloved, unwanted, and incapable of fulfilling my roles as a wife and mother consumed me.

FINANCIAL CRISIS

After our divorce, my ex-husband sought my financial assistance to secure loans from banks in order to settle his company's debts. Despite his heartfelt promises of repayment, he unfortunately failed to fulfill his commitments. Consequently, I found myself sinking deeper into a quagmire of debt, a situation worsened by mounting bank interest. The outstanding amount eventually reached an alarming sum of nearly S$100,000. Our daily existence turned into a constant struggle for survival, teetering on the brink of financial collapse. Life during this period was exceptionally challenging.

As I neglected my dietary habits, my weight steadily increased by approximately eight kilograms. Consequently, my body succumbed to inflammation, leading to excruciating joint pain in both knees. Amid my physical struggles, I stopped caring about my appearance and the way I dressed, which only deepened my sense of despair. Each day became an almost unbearable ordeal, devoid of anticipation or purpose. I had lost all sense of direction and meaning in my life.

PARENTS' CANCER

I had already reached the depths of despair, but life dealt me another cruel blow. In 2017, my mother, already disabled, was diagnosed with stage four breast cancer. Determined to support her recovery, I exhausted my heart and my dwindling savings on her operation, medical treatments, and caregiving.

Within a year of her diagnosis, tragedy struck again. My father was diagnosed with stage four colon cancer. At this time, I was already in a precarious financial situation, but I had no choice but to shoulder the costs of my father's operation, medical needs, and emotional support.

As the emotional and financial pillar for my family, I had to project strength for my parents as they faced their own battles with cancer. Coping with their challenging behaviors proved to be an immense task. Managing their anger, frustration, impatience, complaints, boredom, and constant demands placed an overwhelming burden on my shoulders. The weight of these responsibilities was too much to bear, leading me to break down numerous times and contemplate giving up.

PARENTS' DEATH

Just when I thought I had endured the harshest challenges life had to offer, fate dealt another devastating blow. In April 2021, I was confronted with unimaginable sorrow as both my parents tragically passed away within a short span of just 23 days. The weight of grief and loss bore heavily on my heart, plunging me into a profound state of mourning. Waves of loss washed over me, leaving me shattered, isolated, and sinking even deeper into the abyss of depression. I lost all confidence and struggled to find a reason to continue. Days turned into months as I was engulfed by darkness. Every step forward felt like an insurmountable mountain. The world continued to move around me, leaving me feeling isolated and disconnected.

GLIMMER OF HOPE

Amidst the shadows, a spark of resilience ignited within me. I found solace in my faith and in the deep affection I held for my daughter. The realization that I wanted to offer her a brighter future ignited a new resolve within me. In that moment, a glimmer of hope emerged, providing me the strength and determination to persevere and face the challenges head-on.

Motivated by an inner desire to overcome the depths of my anguish, I turned to self-help literature focused on depression and emotional well-being. Intent on healing my deep-rooted pain and navigating through my grief, I embarked on a journey to reclaim control over my mental health. Gradually, I began to confront the overwhelming sense of worthlessness that had consumed me, taking small but courageous steps to challenge the negative thoughts that had haunted me for so long.

As I journeyed towards healing, I discovered a strength I never knew I possessed. I connected with support groups and found solace in the stories of others who had faced similar battles. Their shared experiences and unwavering support lifted my spirit, helping me realize that I was not alone.

I also learned the importance of self-care and self-compassion. I began to engage in activities that brought me joy and nourished my soul. Writing became my refuge; I poured my heart onto paper, exploring my emotions and embracing vulnerability. Through this, I found a voice to express my pain. As the darkness gradually lifted, I came to understand that my journey was about more than just overcoming depression; it was about reclaiming my life. Armed with newfound determination, I started to rebuild my life by taking on part-time work that provided stability and a sense of purpose.

The road to recovery was far from easy. There were setbacks and moments of doubt, but having witnessed the depths of despair and emerged stronger on the other side, I took heart. Each small victory became a stepping stone, leading me ever closer to a brighter future.

EMOTIONAL WELLNESS

To embark on the journey of rebuilding and moving forward in life, the first step I took was acknowledging the negative emotional state I found myself in. It became increasingly clear to me that merely bouncing back wasn't enough; I needed to make significant strides forward to regain what I had lost and restore my momentum and self-confidence.

With these insights in mind, I began implementing various practices to boost my emotional well-being:

1.   **Promote Feelings of Self-worth**
Recognizing the significance of starting my day on a

positive note, I established a deliberate routine focused on self-affirmation and expressing gratitude towards myself. This practice had a transformative impact on my mood and fostered a sense of self-worth, which in turn amplified my productivity.

2.   Practice Mindfulness

To achieve mindfulness, I made a conscious effort to be fully present. Instead of letting my thoughts wander towards the future or past, I focused solely on the present moment. This approach helped me avoid distraction and maintain mental clarity.

3.   Connection and Communication

I understood that emotional wellness was not just about managing my own emotions, but also about forging meaningful connections with others. Realizing that I didn't have to navigate my journey alone, I bravely opened up and shared my feelings with a trusted friend. This act proved immensely beneficial, offering fresh perspectives, recollections of joyful memories, and even helping me identify silver linings amidst stressful situations. It resulted in a significant improvement in my emotional well-being and bolstered my sense of self-worth.

4.   Stress Management

I actively sought out activities that brought me joy. These included leisurely walks, relaxing baths, rejuvenating massages, karaoke sessions, uplifting movies, and deep-breathing exercises. By incorporating these activities into my routine, I prioritized self-care and cultivated a greater sense of contentment.

5.   Work-Life Balance

To optimize my emotional well-being, I aimed for a healthy balance between work and leisure. Acknowledging the importance of this, I set aside dedicated time for recreational activities such as going to the movies, massages, karaoke, and even occasional shopping trips. These moments of leisure nurtured my emotional state and created space for greater fulfillment.

6.   Good Health Practices

To achieve emotional wellness, I adopted good health practices, which have proven transformative in attaining optimal health, joy, and happiness in my life.

Regular Exercise: Engaging in physical activity on a consistent basis helps me improve cardiovascular health, build strength, enhance flexibility, and boost mood. I find activities I enjoy and make them a regular part of my routine.

Nutrition and Balanced Diet: To nourish my body with a balanced diet, I include a variety of fruits, vegetables, whole grains, lean proteins, and healthy fats in my meals. I limit processed foods, sugary drinks, and excessive salt or saturated fats. I make it a habit to drink an ample amount of water throughout the day to maintain optimal health.

Sufficient Sleep: I plan and prioritize getting an adequate amount of sleep each night. Quality sleep allows my body to rejuvenate, promotes mental clarity, and supports overall well-being.

Regular Health Check-ups: I proactively schedule routine check-ups with healthcare professionals to monitor my health, identify any potential issues early on, and ensure necessary preventive care.

7.   Set Goals

Setting goals had a significant impact on my self-esteem and self-worth. Achieving them brought a sense of accomplishment and validation, which boosted my confidence. I set goals that were realistic yet challenging, tailored to my strengths and capabilities."

CONCLUSION

As I reflect upon my journey, I am filled with a sense of gratitude. The adversities I encountered along the way have molded me into a woman of remarkable resilience. Emerging from the abyss of depression, I bear the marks of my experiences, but I also carry with me profound wisdom and an intensified reverence for life's invaluable moments. Through my own healing, I found the strength to support others on their journeys to recovery.

I have developed a transformative and impactful program called "Unsinkable Faith." This program is designed to guide individuals through a journey of personal growth and transformation. If you're ready to embark on a personal development journey, I warmly invite you to connect with me and explore the profound potential of embracing "Unsinkable Faith." Together, we can unlock the transformative power within you.

ABOUT CAROLLYNE TONG

Carollyne Tong holds a Master's degree in International Business and a Bachelor's degree in Commerce. She is a certified WSQ ACLP trainer and a Style Coach. She has developed acclaimed programs such as "Unsinkable Faith" and "90/90 Marriage", which are designed with effective strategies to empower individuals to boost their self-confidence and encourage healthier relationships. These programs enable individuals to excel in both life and business. To learn more about Carollyne and her work, connect with her at https://www.linktr.ee/carollynetong.

11

Overcoming Depression after Losing my Dad

By Hisham Ahmad

Depression is an illness characterized by persistent sadness and a loss of interest in activities that you normally enjoy. It's also marked by an inability to carry out daily activities, for at least two weeks. Have you ever been in such situations? Many have, right?

This condition came upon me in my younger days when I was 15 years old. I just didn't pay attention when my father, who was in a terminal state, called me. "Son, can you call the barber to come to our house and cut my hair?" he asked.

I simply ignored his request and continued playing my mobile game. And when my mum asked what my father had asked me to do, I mumbled, saying it was nothing important. I never knew what the consequences would be after he passed away.

This isn't a horror movie narrative. It's something else entirely.

My name is Hisham, and I want to share my story of depression with you. In a matter of a few days, he, sadly, passed away. Soon after, I found myself grappling with an overwhelming sadness, an effect that introduced me to the term "Depression". This happened when we were still living in Ang Mo Kio, a residential town in Singapore.

One morning, I woke up and sat still, consumed by thoughts of how I was going to guide and help my family. I was only 15, but I found myself considering whether I could handle and assume the responsibilities of a father figure.

I was just a kid, still growing up, and I needed to enjoy life. But as the saying goes, "Let go and let God". He will arrange everything for you, so don't worry. But if you overthink, it can overwhelm your mind and lead to depression. It makes you ruminate on the missing figure in your life, in my case, my father. I found myself constantly thinking, "Why did he leave me and us so soon?"

For days, I've been in my bedroom, contemplating whether I should continue studying or stop and find a job to support my mom in our journey forward into the future.

I started asking friends if they had any work experience or knew of any jobs. Soon, the notion of "working" began to occupy my mind after hearing from my friends. A few days later, having considered the idea of a job, I mustered up the courage to ask my mom for permission to look for a job with a friend.

She became worried, questioning why I wanted to stop studying and start working. In response, I politely explained that I wanted to help stabilize our family's income. She insisted, in a stern tone, that there was no need for that, as she had plans for us. But I persisted.

My repeated requests started to annoy her. Once again, albeit slightly agitated, she told me that I should continue studying because it would ensure a better future for me. Feeling disappointed, I responded, "OK, mom."

I wasn't in the mood for breakfast, and my mom asked me why I wasn't eating. I remained silent, stood up, and walked away, grabbing my bag to go to school. Deep down, she knew that I wanted to work and help the family since dad had passed away.

In her silence, she contemplated finding a stall to rent and becoming a hawker just to support our family.

When I got back from school, she approached me and reassured me that I didn't need to worry about the family's expenses, as she was working out a solution. In my silence, I began to follow my friend who worked as a cleaner. I despised the job at first, but seeing the money I earned made me smile, and this motivated me to continue working.

Soon, after a few weeks, my mom started her stall at Whampoa Market, Block 92. Everything else fell into place from there. She reassured me that it was okay, that my brother was helping her out. After school, I could come and help on the weekends, but once I finished my studies, she encouraged me to find a job as it would contribute towards my CPF (Central Provident Fund). That's when my depression started to fade away slowly. I received the green light from my mother to stop at 'O' Levels and start working.

And that's how the story unfolds...

About Hisham Ahmad

Hisham Ahmad guides individuals on achieving financial prosperity while also balancing quality family time by helping them gain self-awareness and discover their potential. Check out his profile at https://linktr.ee/sham71ig

12

Work in Progress

By Fazal Ahamed

True to form, I'll keep this write-up brief. Delving deeply into my journey might stir up emotions, which is something I want to avoid. In fact, just the thought of being emotionally triggered is already causing me some distress.

How and when did it all begin?

I believe depression takes hold when the mind is trapped in the past trauma or consumed by worries about the future. I experienced both.

I guess it started when I was a child. Growing up as a shy kid, my parents got separated and remarried to different partners. My mom had an affair with my dads sisters husband and she got married to him. They did this for financial benefits. Later, he divorced my mom and he went back to his first wife, but they both continue the affair till date, under the sheets

This ignited a series of catastrophic events (domino effect) and my life crumbled like a house of cards.

I had to leave home when I was 13 and have been alone, hustling without any form of support or backup (emotional, financial, psychological) since then. Eventually, my dad also got married to another women to complicate the situation for me. Additionally, I lost my lifetime savings and inheritance because of trusting a dysfunctional family.

When the family broke, it became like a civil war situation.
1. Parents lost interest in me and they focussed on their new life with their new partners. As a result, I was deprived of the essential family ambience which lead to many other complications.
2. Relatives / outsiders, interfered and exploited the situation of the broken family to make things worse.

It became a situation of financial abuse. To help themselves and to help me, I only had two requests to them.
1. Please own up to recover the assets and undo the damage / loss inflicted upon me.
2. If they are not capable of recovering the assets / undoing the loss, at least try to preserve and grow whatever is left and pass it on me.

My cries and plea for help fell into deaf ears and everyone involved were indifferent to the whole situation. In fact, they had no regrets of destroying a lineage and ruining my life.

How did I identify it was depression?

I realized it when I experienced rapid aging. Even though I'm currently 35, my biological age feels like 55. Within a span of just three years, all the strands of hair on my head, face, and body turned white. To put it in perspective, it's similar to running a marathon or sprint where you don't feel discomfort until a few days after the race. The cramps and pain suddenly appear and grow exponentially.

Additionally, I spent over a decade in a haze, avoiding anything that reminded me of home. Naturally, this had a domino effect on my career and professional life, making things even worse.

It dawned upon me that I should have born in a better setup which was at least capable of providing the basic family architecture. But, do I have a choice on this?

How did depression affect me?

The sequence of events ensured that I started my life from a point much below ground zero, in negative territory. I understand that many people start from zero, but my situation felt even worse because I had a dysfunctional family that continuously inflicted damage. It felt like trying to fill a leaking bucket. No matter how hard I tried to make progress and fill the bucket, it would always leak out due to its holes. Sometimes, I even felt that having no family at all would be better than enduring this.

Dysfunctional family, lack of money, loss of inheritance (although I had it until a few years ago), a broken career, absence of valid skill sets, no special talents, and poor health. It's all piling up on me.

I genuinely fear that I might end up homeless and won't be able to afford even the basic necessities to sustain my life. However, I am actively working towards changing this situation.

When people hear my full story and learn about how I lost everything, many of them ask, "Bro, why is your life so cursed?"

How am I dealing with it?

Even though it may appear as a train wreck from the outside, I believe I have a guardian angel who makes things easier for me. I am always grateful for that support, and it simply works.

I am intentionally disconnecting from everything and everyone that carries traces of my past life.

Additionally, I have made the decision to not have a family of my own. This means my lineage will end with me, and I won't have children. I don't believe I will ever find or meet a partner, and even if I am ready, it might be too late. I have accepted this reality and come to terms with it, although it was very difficult.

How am I overcoming depression?

The "M" word - I turned to prayer and meditation. I have been initiated into it, and I now practice powerful breathwork and meditation techniques. Whenever I engage in these practices, I feel a sense of euphoria and invincibility because it helps to create a distance between me and myself. It's like getting high on life and forgetting about the train wreck that surrounds me. It feels like experiencing a new birth.

Although I have received advice to take anti-depressants, I choose to avoid them. Instead, I strive to remain consistent with my meditation practices, hoping that they will continue to be my source of healing and growth.

Additionally, I am striving to set goals and milestones in all aspects of my life, actively pursuing them. This is especially true when it comes to transforming my current financial situation. I aim to leave behind a substantial legacy that can benefit people for many generations.

What lessons have I learned?

I have come to realize that I am merely a small speck in this vast universe. Every day, I wake up and strive to do my best with a smile on my face.

Meditation has been instrumental in teaching me these lessons. Here's a crash course that I remind myself of every day before my meditation practice:

1. All rules in this existence are my rules.
2. "This moment is all there is " - accepting the present as it is and it cannot be any other way.
3. My ability to respond is limitless.
4. I am not the body; I am not even the mind.
5. Be a mother to the world.

Any advice for the reader?

At the risk of sounding preachy, consider this: The world outside is already tough and let's try to make it easy by practicing kindness and empathy.

Plus, If every breath you take is blissful, and every moment you live becomes a celebration, would you still need extraordinary experiences? Sometimes, finding joy in the simple act of breathing and embracing the present moment can bring profound fulfillment. Look within yourself and cultivate a mindset that allows you to appreciate the beauty of ordinary experiences. In doing so, you may find that true happiness lies in the small, everyday moments that often go unnoticed.

About Fazal Ahamed

Fazal Ahamed humbly describes himself as nobody special. However, if there is still an interest in connecting with him, his LinkedIn profile can be found at the following link: https://www.linkedin.com/in/fazalahamed/

13

From Darkness I Saw Light

By Rajalakshmi Jeyabalan

As I sat on the edge of my queen-size bed by the tall window facing my driveway, hoping for more light to seep in, a thought came to me: "I am lost, I can't feel myself."

My emotions were jaded, as blank as a pristine sheet of paper with no words penned upon it. There was no story to narrate, no success to celebrate as victory, no salt, sugar, or spice to create any semblance of excitement, even in a dish. I was a shell of blankness on the outside, even as chaos roiled within. The only urge was to cut through this blankness from inside out.

I stood up, made my way to the kitchen, and pulled out a knife. I prepared to slice into my arm, the nearest thing I could find to the blank piece of paper I felt like—craving to feel the emotions of words.

But I hesitated, caught between my physical reality and the horrifying possibility of the consequences if I did successfully break through the silent chaos within me. Suddenly, the piercing cries of my three-month-old daughter shattered the silence, snapping me out of my suicidal trance.

I dropped the knife onto the kitchen countertop and sprinted towards my child, who had awoken from her prolonged nap. As I held her in my arms, bottle-feeding her, I realized that I had been in this state of illusion before, but never this deep and low. It was a place of familiarity, reminiscent of my first pregnancy four years ago. But this time, it was harder to swim back up to the surface. Although I could join the dots and recognize this as a familiar post-pregnancy phase, sitting by the window and feeling trapped had a much stronger sense of familiarity.

My ex-husband suggested I start attending moms' playgroups or initiate an exercise regimen to get more endorphins and dopamine into my system, to activate my happy hormones and keep myself active. I was fortunate to find a gym facility a stone's throw away from home that hosted both a moms' playgroup and fitness classes which offered childcare while the mothers worked out. I was overjoyed to begin feeling better from within and to socialize again like I used to in my corporate job prior to my second pregnancy.

The happiness I found from socializing and the rush I felt after a great cardio workout seemed wonderful at first, but soon started to feel like short-term gratifications. On days when it rained or during long weekend holidays when I had no gym or social events to escape to, I felt an absence of external validation.

The pattern of sitting by the window, hoping for better days, returned. This time, I found myself demanding to be left alone by loved ones and not to be interrupted as I sat on my bed, staring through the window onto the driveway.

One day, as I was strolling along the school corridor, pushing the stroller carrying my six-month-old child deep in slumber, I waited to pick up my oldest daughter from kindergarten. As I did, I found myself mentally zoning out, contemplating my future and searching for solutions.

I had ticked off several boxes: Yes, I was fitter now; yes, I had lost weight and almost returned to my pre-pregnancy self; yes, I was financially well provided for by my husband; yes, I had a house and two beautiful children. But despite all this, I couldn't understand why I still felt trapped.

A school mom, whom I had become acquainted with, nudged me out of my daydreaming state and asked if I would like to tag along for a Business Mindset Workshop. I leaped at the opportunity to attend, viewing this as a new event camouflaged as an escape from my current reality.

Little did I know that I would hear the pivotal phrase, "What is your innermost dominating thought?" during the workshop.

I walked out of the workshop with that sentence buzzing in my mind, and I kept wondering: Wow, what is my mind telling me without my conscious knowledge?

This was the beginning of a whole new journey for me, which was called Inner Child Shadow Work.

This workshop served as an initiator, only scratching the surface of my patterns of chaos.

When I delved into deeper inner work, my subconscious mind transported me back to a moment when I was seated on a bed in a dark room, at the age of five.

It was my parents' second housewarming party. In an attempt to persuade me to stay with them from then on, instead of with my paternal grandmother, my father led me to a room which he introduced as mine, with a humble smile.

He turned on the light and told me that my two older sisters would be sleeping beside me and that they would always be with me from now on. The term 'sisters' was new to my young mind. To exacerbate the feeling of "I don't belong in this family" was my father, who seemed like a complete stranger. As a five-year-old, no one I valued had formally introduced this balding man, who had a darker complexion than me and bore no resemblance to me, as my father—an important masculine figure in my life.

Without fear, I turned to him and said, "I am going to my home with my grandmother."

His humble smile began to fade, and he seemed more unpredictable to me than before. He ushered me onto the queen-sized bed that was set on the floor, turned off the light, and closed the door, locking it from the outside.

The room was pitch dark, and I sat in the corner of the bed, staring at the thin strip of white light seeping in from the gap under the door.

Five minutes of silence, being locked in the room, felt like five hours of entrapment. In this solitude, I had programmed my mind to believe, "I am stuck and will never be rescued."

When the hypnotherapist helped me connect the emotion to the words, I had an epiphany: this is why

I could never feel comfortable in moments of solitude and peace.

Through timeline therapy, which focuses on trauma, I was guided to connect the dots of patterns in moments where I always felt the urge to break free when in solitude but remained stuck due to the overwhelming feeling.

Part of the trauma rewiring process involved removing the pattern of stagnancy, which was also causing a lack of physical movement. This process allowed me to break free from patterns of escapism, as I no longer felt the need to flee in moments of peace. Instead, I chose to remain in moments of progress and growth.

Depression is now a thing of the past for me. Since 2019, I realized that many of my choices were made out of a sense of familiarity with trauma-bonded relationships. The choices of clothes, job scopes, friends, even the houses I bought were transitions in my healing journey, emerging from my inner child wounds that manifested as patterns in my adulthood.

If not for the depression I experienced, I would not have slowed down in my reality, which provided a much-needed rest from the limiting beliefs that ruled my life. Depression was a deep state of rest that my greater good needed, allowing me to walk through the path of darkness and see that there is so much more light waiting to shine from within the darkness I feared to seek.

Indeed, there is light at the end of the tunnel, a light that will never dim once it's found.

About Rajalakshmi Jeyabalan

Rajalakshmi Jeyabalan has been a Certified Reiki Master since 2019 and a Certified Instructor of Subconscious Behavioural Mind Reprogramming since 2020. Currently residing in Perth, Australia, she conducts online meditation sessions and shares insights into cosmic alignment using astrology, along with brain and heart coherence techniques to channel the current energy shifts for her followers. Her niche lies in guiding her clients to delve into their past life karmic patterns or Akashic Records, helping them understand their true soul purpose and mission on Earth in this birth.

Instagram: @rajijeyanair
Tiktok: @rajijeyanair
Facebook: Raji Rajalakshmi Jeyabalan

14

You are GOOD enough!

By Allie Ng

I am now 46 years old, and as I reflect upon my journey, I am reminded of the battles I have faced with anxiety since childhood. Throughout my adult years, whenever life's difficulties arose, anxiety and depression would intertwine, leaving me feeling overwhelmed.

One significant thread woven into the fabric of my existence is my relationship with my mother, a relationship that has been fraught with tension since my early years. As the eldest daughter among nine siblings, my mother endured a turbulent upbringing. Verbal and physical abuse were constant companions, inflicted upon her by my grandmother. Without a clear understanding of what love truly meant, my mother carried deep emotional insecurities within her, leading to a strong inclination to control people, possessions, and even money. Moreover, her relationship with my father lacked harmony, further fueling her dissatisfaction, which often found its release in the form of venting her frustrations upon her children.

Inheriting my grandmother's parenting style, my mother wielded her own weapons, not leaving visible marks but causing profound damage to our developing personalities. Verbal violence became her chosen method, incessantly belittling and diminishing us. Her words echoed in our minds like a broken record, repeating hurtful insults that diminished our sense of self-worth. The constant barrage of emotional abuse left me feeling worthless, as if I were an existence beneath even the lowest of standards.

My mother's emotions were volatile, leaving my younger brother and me in a constant state of apprehension. He once described it by saying, "I feel like a lamb living next to a lion, never knowing when she will unleash her anger. I sit in stillness, waiting for the impending doom."

Furthermore, my mother exhibited a clear favoritism toward males over females, intensifying the strictness of her discipline upon me as the eldest daughter. Each day, my mother, lost in the chaos of her own emotions, hurled curses at us, filling her language with embarrassing insults such as, "You are so useless, you should go die," or "You are worthless, go be a prostitute."

This cycle of verbal and emotional abuse persisted relentlessly, cementing the belief within me that I was truly inferior, a being worse than garbage. The weight of these unbearable insults clung to my psyche, haunting me well into adulthood.

Every child yearns for recognition and praise from their parents, and I, too, sought validation. Throughout my school years, I strived tirelessly to achieve excellent grades, even becoming the top student in my university class and receiving the honor of the most outstanding student in my faculty upon graduation. Yet, even with these accomplishments, I dared not invite my family to my graduation ceremony. The belief that I was not good enough in my mother's eyes consumed me.

The deep-rooted subconscious belief that "I am not good enough" permeated my being, causing overwhelming anxiety and insecurity. I lived in constant fear that my flaws and imperfections would disappoint others, resulting in a self-imposed distance from those around me. Building genuine connections became a formidable challenge as my fear of being hurt prevented me from fully embracing the potential for meaningful relationships.

As an adult, my romantic relationships mirrored the tumultuous nature of my upbringing. My insecurities rendered me overly dependent on my partners, yet my controlling and perfectionist tendencies compelled me to incessantly focus on their perceived flaws. Consequently, I found myself relentlessly criticizing my partners, unable to recognize and appreciate their positive qualities.

At the age of 32, a pivotal moment arose when my then-boyfriend uttered a statement that struck me to my core: "Why do you always focus on the negative aspects of me? Can't you see the good in me?" It was at that juncture that I resolved to seek psychological therapy, recognizing the need to confront the deep-seated wounds that haunted me.

Following an evaluation, I was informed that I was a "survivor of verbal abuse and emotional neglect." I was subsequently referred to a clinical psychologist at a government childhood trauma center for specialized treatment.

Embarking on this therapeutic journey marked my first experience of receiving psychological support. My therapist extended care and compassion, fostering an environment of trust between us. Although I eventually completed my therapy at the childhood trauma center, I maintained contact with my therapist, unaware of the unforeseen turn our relationship would take. Over time, he confessed his feelings for me, and our connection blossomed into a romantic partnership.

However, our path together was met with an unexpected obstacle when a third party entered the picture. The therapist, torn between the choices before him, insisted on ending our relationship to be with the third party. I found myself unable to accept this outcome, as he had become the sole source of trust within my world. Believing it was my own inadequacy and unworthiness that drove him away, I spiraled into a state of extreme anxiety and severe depression. Ultimately, in a moment of profound despair, I made a desperate attempt to end my own life.

Following the harrowing incident, I received psychiatric medication to address my mental health. However, the side effects proved unbearable for my physical well-being. It was through the help of Chinese medicine that I began to slowly regain balance, nurturing both my mental and physical states. Nonetheless, as the root cause of my depression remained unaddressed, each encounter with life's challenges threatened to drag me back into the depths of despair.

In my quest for healing and self-exploration, I devoted years of my life, from the ages of 35 to 39, to various body-mind-spirit therapies in Hong Kong. Sound therapy, mindfulness meditation, and countless other methods were explored, yet my persistent sleep disorder remained unaffected.

At the age of 39, I made the bold decision to quit my job and seek solace in Taiwan. Living there on a tourist visa for six years, I immersed myself in a plethora of body-mind-spirit therapies. While I invested significant time and financial resources into these endeavors, it wasn't until I encountered a German quantum instrument called the Timewaver that a profound realization unfolded. I began to understand that all bodily ailments, including my insomnia, were mere "results" of deeper beliefs within me. Merely addressing the symptoms would yield only temporary effects. If true and lasting transformation was to occur, it was imperative to confront the core beliefs themselves.

One of the fundamental beliefs that gripped my being was the conviction that "I am worthless, useless, and hold no value." It became evident that my anxiety and depression were manifestations of this belief, taking root within my physical body. Consequently, when life events triggered this belief, such as encountering relationship problems that echoed my childhood experiences of feeling abandoned and worthless, I would spiral into severe anxiety and depression.

Individuals burdened with feelings of inferiority and low self-esteem tend to manifest two distinct patterns. The first involves a paralyzing fear of failure, resulting in a complete aversion to exploring new endeavors. The second pattern encompasses an incessant drive to improve oneself, driven by the misguided notion that worthiness and love can only be earned through constant self-improvement. Yet, this perpetual effort often leads to an unhealthy state of "trying too hard" and extreme perfectionism, ultimately cornering oneself in an unattainable quest for validation.

If you find yourself resonating with the second pattern, feeling the incessant need to constantly prove your worth through tireless self-improvement, I implore you to listen closely: "You are already enough, and there is no need to try so hard." It is perfectly okay to release the weight of constant striving because the truth is, you are not the problem. The real issue lies in the fact that you have been trying too hard. It is time to remember that even without pushing yourself to extremes, even with imperfections and vulnerabilities, you are still deserving of love.

Just a few days ago, while I was immersed in meditation, a powerful image emerged. I realized that whenever I resist certain aspects of my life, such as falling ill, an instant surge of anger erupts within me. I despise myself for not being healthy enough and resent my perceived weakness. In that moment, I saw myself taking a sharp blade and repeatedly stabbing it into my own heart, fueled by an immense anger that sought to destroy me.

Over the past two decades, I have exhausted my resources, be it time, money, or energy, in a relentless pursuit to fix that imperfect version of myself. But what ultimately saved me was a simple realization: I do not need to do anything more. I merely have to release the blade, accept all facets of myself, and stop resisting.

As this thought coursed through me, an overwhelming wave of sadness washed over me. A gentle voice whispered, "God never punishes you. Why do you constantly punish yourself?"

In light of my journey and personal growth, I would like to share the beautiful words of a dear friend who has also traversed the depths of depression:

"Instead of continually trying to 'fix' yourself, embrace the mindset of unconditional acceptance. Love and restore yourself without any expectations or deadlines. This is where true healing begins.

Acceptance is the key that prevents you from pushing yourself to the brink. Embrace acceptance and find solace in the cold winter, resting until you feel replenished. Allow yourself the time to wonder when it is right to emerge and witness the vibrant world once more. Without forcing yourself or yielding to external pressures, you will instinctively know when the time is right. Curiosity will ignite within you, and motivation will flow naturally. It is as simple as that."

Dear reader, if you find yourself entangled in the grip of depression, remember that you do not need to continually strive to fix yourself. Embrace acceptance, practice self-love, and allow yourself the time and space to heal. Know that you are deserving of love and that fundamental changes come from within, from a place of self-acceptance and self-compassion.

May you find solace in embracing your worthiness, releasing the burden of self-imposed expectations, and nurturing yourself with love and acceptance. The world awaits your renewed spirit, and the journey ahead beckons with the promise of joy and fulfillment.

About Allie Ng

Meet Allie Ng, a passionate Hongkonger who wears multiple hats with grace and expertise. As an Advanced Instructor of Pastel Nagomi Art, she guides and inspires others on a colorful journey of self-expression and self-acceptance. In addition, Allie serves as a skilled Facilitator of Wealth & Joy Simulation, helping individuals unlock their full potential in both abundance and happiness. With an insatiable curiosity, she fearlessly explores the depths of the subconscious, delving into the mysteries of the human psyche. For inquiries and connections, reach out to Allie at allieng336@gmail.com. Stay updated with her artistic endeavors and transformative insights by visiting her Facebook fanpage at https://www.facebook.com/alliepastelnagomi and following her on IG at allie.ananda.

15

This Palette of Madness

By Janice Sheilah

Look at me.
Because
I used to be young.
I used to be a winner.
I used to be someone that mattered.

I used to be that person who succeeded at anything she set her mind on. I used to be that person who drove the bus that left a minute early and everyone had to take a backseat. Everyone missed the ride.

Well, I have bad news for you. I'm no longer that person. Or so, I think.

I'm not here to write about how I overcame myself and my inadequacies. I haven't.

This is an ongoing battle, this battle I have with myself.

There are days when I'm waiting in the shadows, staring into space, my mind blank, my heart bleeding deeply. I go through days like any normal human being, but the darkness and the turmoil I feel inside are relentless, wild and searing. No one sees it, but I know it's there. I hate the lies I tell myself that things will get better. They hardly ever do. I go to bed troubled, tired and anxious. Sleep may overcome me, but it's a wash-rinse-repeat cycle all over again as soon as I wake up the next day.

I carry this huge and heavy weight on my shoulders and I don't even know what it is and why I've lugged it around for over 4 decades. Here's a list of what I've tried:

I did meditation.
I attended transcendental courses.
I went to the gym seven days a week, 4 weeks a month and worked out for at least 2-3 hours.
I tried escapism.
I turned to religion.
I talked to a mind coach.
I tried veganism.
I contacted my guardian angels.
I stalked and befriended my exes to gain closure.
I deleted toxic people from my circle of existence.

The things I didn't dare try were suicide, doing drugs, hiring a shrink and being on medication. I'm scared of pain and I don't have the money to hire someone who doesn't really listen to what I don't say.

"You cannot have depression. You have a child!"
Well, ma'am, sir I do.

"How can you be depressed? You've led a sheltered and privileged life!"
Do wealth and privilege exempt me from it? Do money, education and a life of ease keep depression at bay?

Sometimes I have happy days. I wake up feeling light, bright and winning. Then as soon as I rise from my bed, BAM! Reality hits me hard. My thoughts immediately get entangled in an intricate web of who I really am and how I should be as the world expects me to be.

We do have only one life, but I feel as if I have squandered half of it already and then someday, I will only be a distant memory. I feel like an artwork waiting to happen - a heady mix of palettes all packed up, waiting to explode into a colourful painting of shades and shadows.

Do I need help? If I do, how do I get it?

One day, once anything here makes any sense to you, could you let me know what you see? You don't have to be a Vermeer or a Van Gogh to unearth the meaning underneath the abrasion so you can understand the abstraction. Just:

Look at me.
Because
I used to be young.
I used to be a winner.
I used to be someone that mattered.

About Janice Sheilah

Janice Sheilah writes about other things too. Follow her on Twitter at @janicesheilah and check out her blog at janicesheilah.wordpress.com

9 789811 878312